Antonín
DVOŘÁK

Te Deum
Op. 103 / B. 176

(Josef Suk)

Vocal Score
Klavierauszug

SERENISSIMA MUSIC, INC.

CONTENTS

1. Te Deum Laudamus 3

2. Tu Rex Gloriæ 13

3. Aeterna Fac cum Sanctis 20

4. Dignare Domine 27

ORCHESTRA

2 Flutes, 2 Oboes, English Horn, 2 Clarinets, 2 Bassoons
4 Horns, 2 Trumpets, 3 Trombones, Tuba
Timpani, Triangle, Bass Drum, Cymbals
Violin I, Violin II, Viola, Violoncello, Double Bass

Duration: ca. 20 minutes
First performance: 21 October, 1892
New York Hall, New York
Antonin Dvorak, conductor

Complete orchestral parts compatible with this vocal score are available (Cat. No. A2594) from
E. F. Kalmus & Co., Inc.
6403 West Rogers Circle
Boca Raton, FL 33487 USA
(800) 434 - 6340
www.kalmus-music.com

Te Deum
Op. 103 / B. 176

1. Te Deum Laudamus

Antonín Dvořák
Piano reduction by Josef Suk
Edited by Carl Simpson

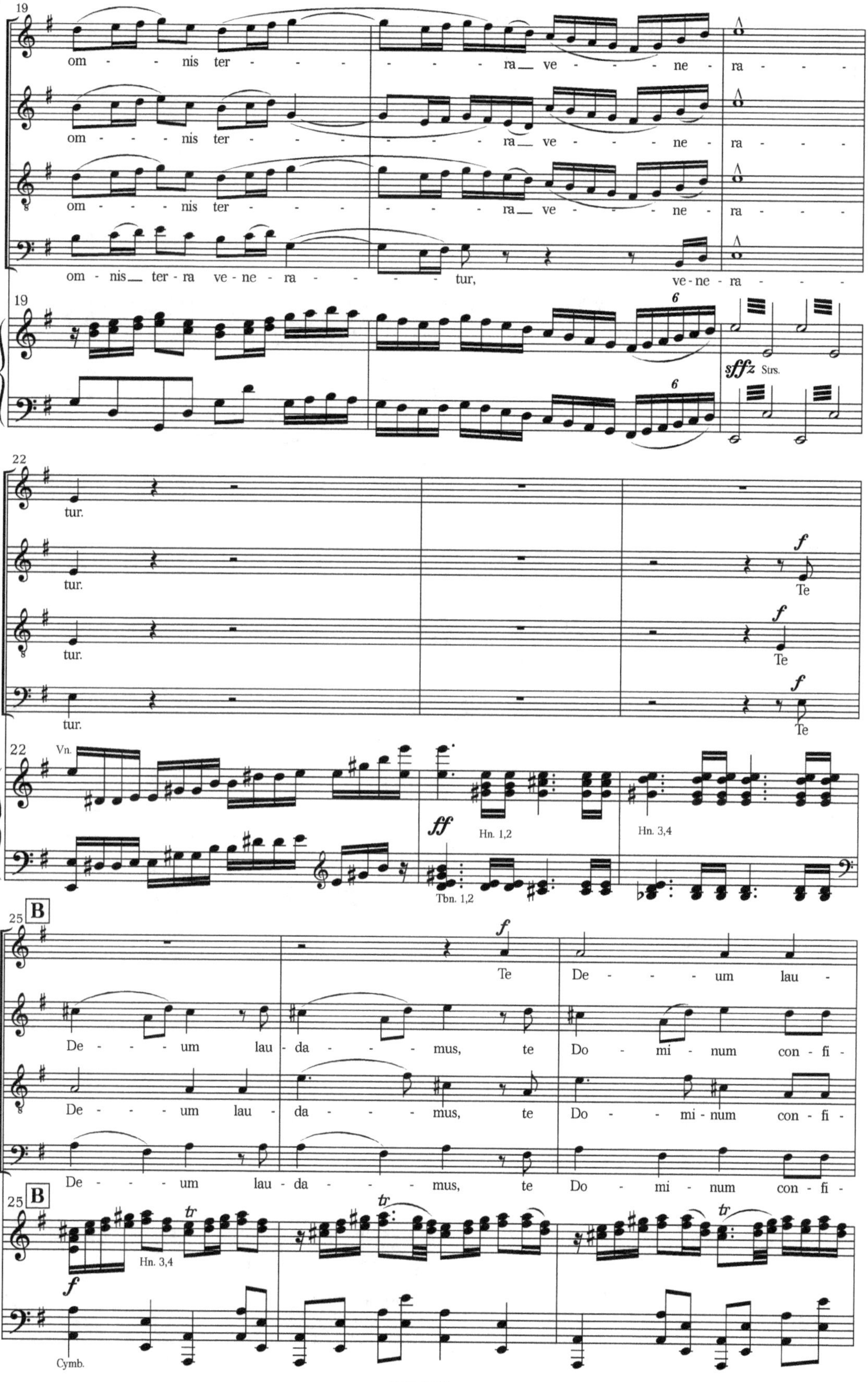
19
om - - nis ter - - - - - - - ra ve - - - ne - ra - - - -
om - - nis ter - - - - - - - ra ve - - - ne - ra - - - -
om - - nis ter - - - - - - - ra ve - - - ne - ra - - - -
om - nis ter-ra ve-ne-ra - - - - tur, ve-ne-ra - - - -
6
sffz Strs.
22
tur.
tur. Te
tur. Te
tur. Te
Vn.
ff
Hn. 1,2
Hn. 3,4
Tbn. 1,2
B
25
Te De - - - um lau -
De - - um lau-da - - - mus, te Do - mi - num con-fi -
De - - um lau - da - - - mus, te Do - - mi-num con-fi -
De - - um lau-da - - - mus, te Do - mi - num con-fi -
Hn. 3,4
Cymb.

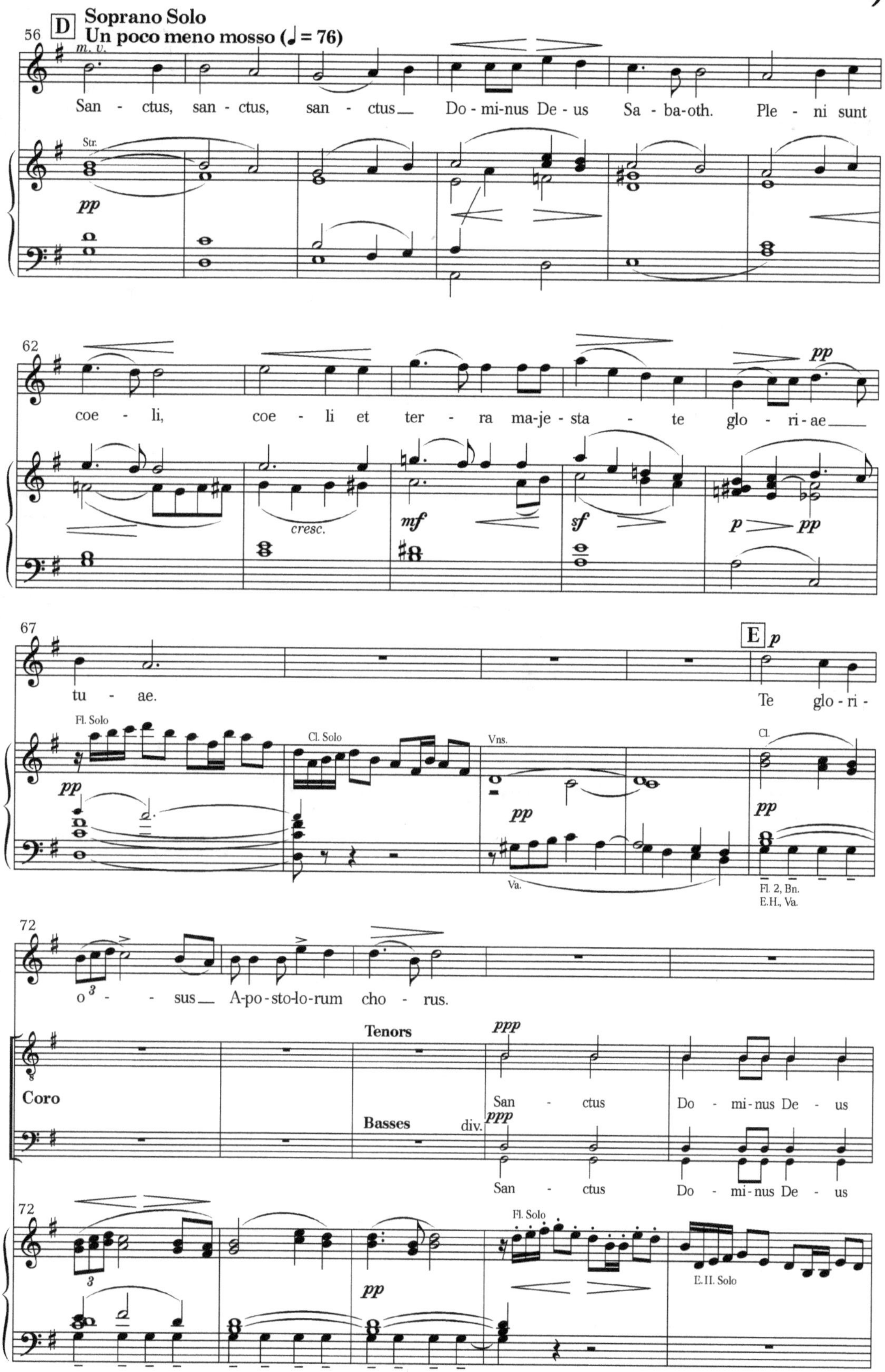
D
Soprano Solo
Un poco meno mosso (♩ = 76)
56
m. v.
San - ctus, san - ctus, san - ctus Do - mi - nus De - us Sa - ba - oth. Ple - ni sunt
Str.
pp
62
coe - li, coe - li et ter - ra ma - je - sta - te glo - ri - ae
pp
cresc.
mf
sf
p
pp
67
tu - ae.
E
p
Te glo - ri -
Fl. Solo
Cl. Solo
Vns.
Cl.
pp
Va.
Fl. 2, Bn.
E.H., Va.
72
o - sus A - po - sto - lo - rum cho - rus.
Tenors
ppp
San - ctus Do - mi - nus De - us
Coro
Basses
div.
ppp
San - ctus Do - mi - nus De - us
72
Fl. Solo
pp
E.H. Solo

2. Tu Rex Gloriæ

3. Aeterna Fac cum Sanctis

4. Dignare Domine

www.ingramcontent.com/pod-product-compliance
Lightning Source LLC
Chambersburg PA
CBHW081025040426
42444CB00014B/3350